Fisher-Price®

Little People®
TODDLER WORKBOOK

PAGES
Numbers
Fun
TEAR OUT

Written by Lauri Posner, M.S. Ed.
Educational Consultant, Robyn Ulzheimer

Cover illustration by Pattie Silver-Thompson
Interior illustrations by Georgene Griffin

Modern Publishing
A Division of Unisystems, Inc.
New York, New York 10022
Printed in the U.S.A.

DEAR PARENTS,

The Fisher-Price® Little People® Toddler Workbooks are an educational way to introduce your child to basic concepts. Research shows that encouraging learning at home has an important influence on your child's future success in school.

Following are some suggestions to keep in mind when using this book:

• Read through the book once, without your child. Cut out the manipulatives on the back pages and have them available for your child to use with selected activities. Many of the manipulatives can also be used as flash cards to reinforce learning.
• Choose a time in the day when your child is alert and able to focus. Limit the amount of time that you use these activities. This should be fun, and not work, for your child.
• Have a selection of pencils and crayons nearby.
• Ask questions of your child to prompt more meaningful learning. For example, when working on the "2" page, ask your child to find things that come in "2s" in your home. (For example, 2 socks, 2 eyes, etc.) Extend the activities beyond the books whenever possible. Ask your child to count groups of objects in their own environment at other times during the day.

Most of all, have fun with the book and enjoy the time you spend with your child.

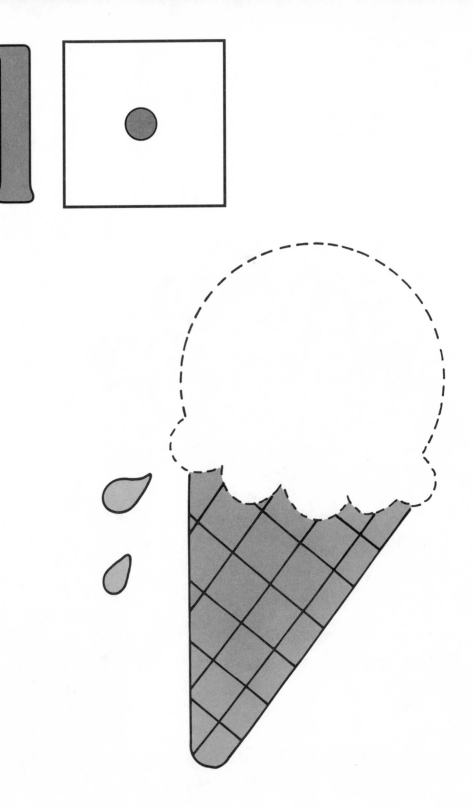

Can you find the picture of 1 scoop of ice cream to put on the cone?

2

Can you find the picture of 2 shoes to put on the girl?

3

Can you find the picture of 3 pigs to put on the farm?

Can you find the picture of 4 shovels to put in the sandbox?

Can you find the picture of 5 tools to put on the workbench?

6

Can you find the picture of 6 beach balls to put on the beach?

Can you find the picture of 7 necklaces to put in the jewelry box?

Can you find the picture of 8 bees to fly in the sky?

Can you find the picture of 9 apples to put under the tree?

10

Can you find the picture of 10 fish to swim in the pond?

Matching Numbers

1

4

Can you draw a line to match the number with the picture showing that same number?

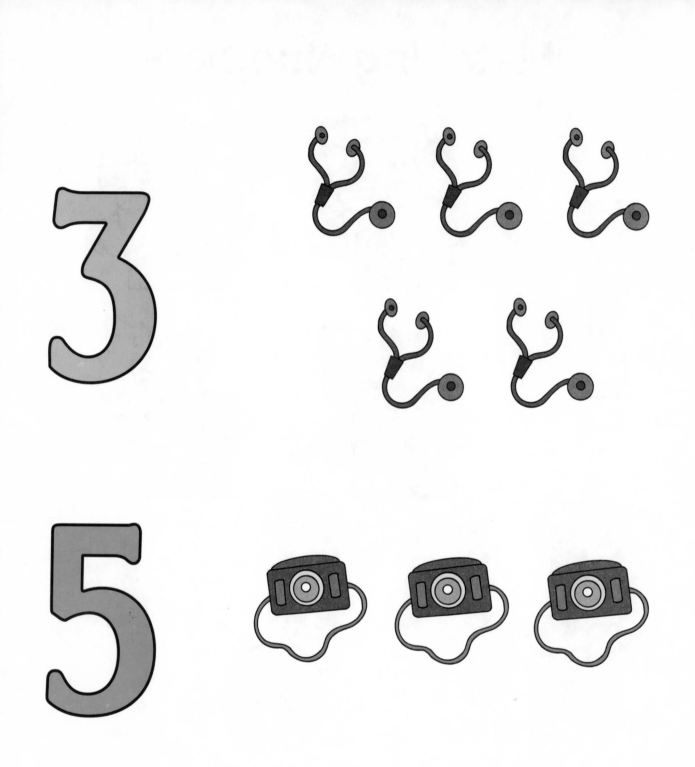

Can you draw a line to match the number with the picture showing that same number?

Counting

How many oranges do you see? Count them.
How many apples do you see? Count them.

Dominoes

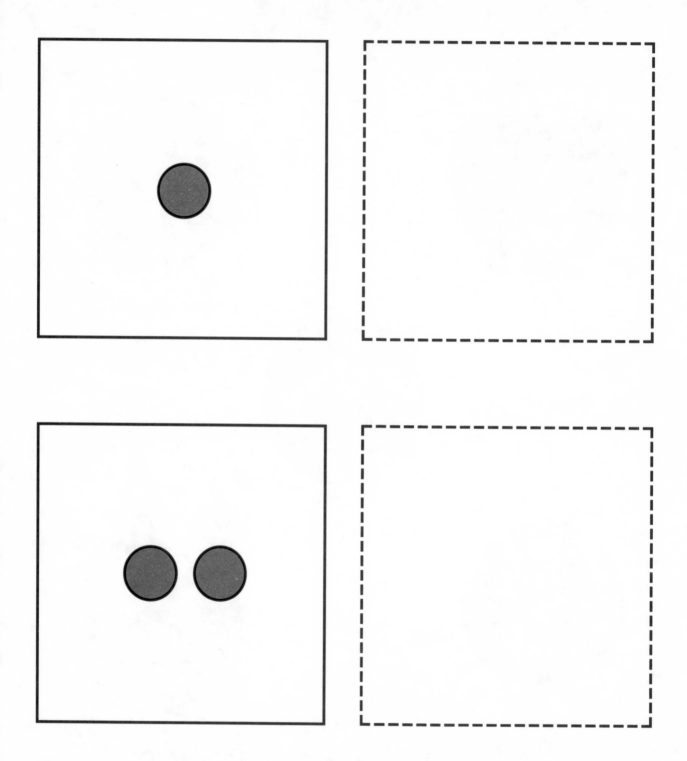

Count the dots in the squares. Can you find the
cut-out card with the same number of dots?
Place the correct card next to the box.

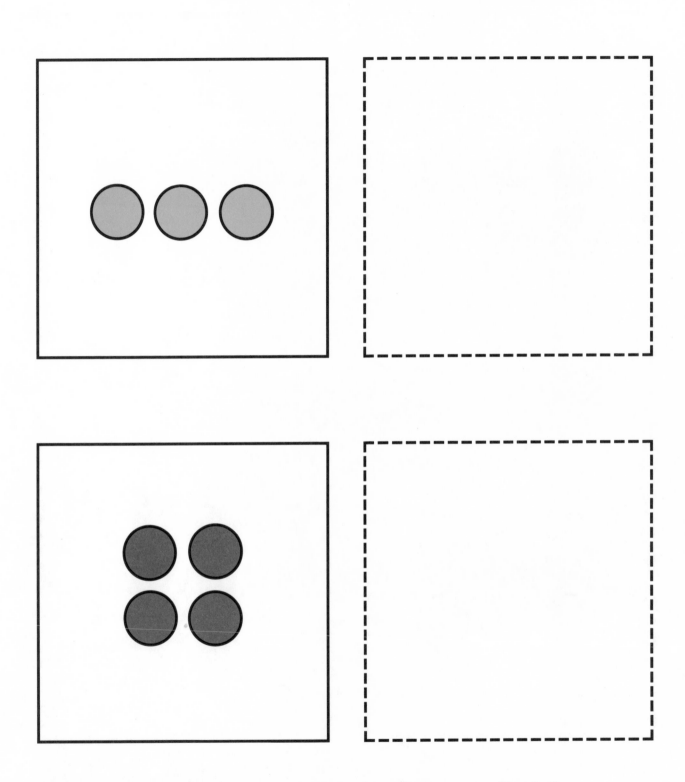

Count the dots in the squares. Can you find the cut-out card with the same number of dots? Place the correct card next to the box.

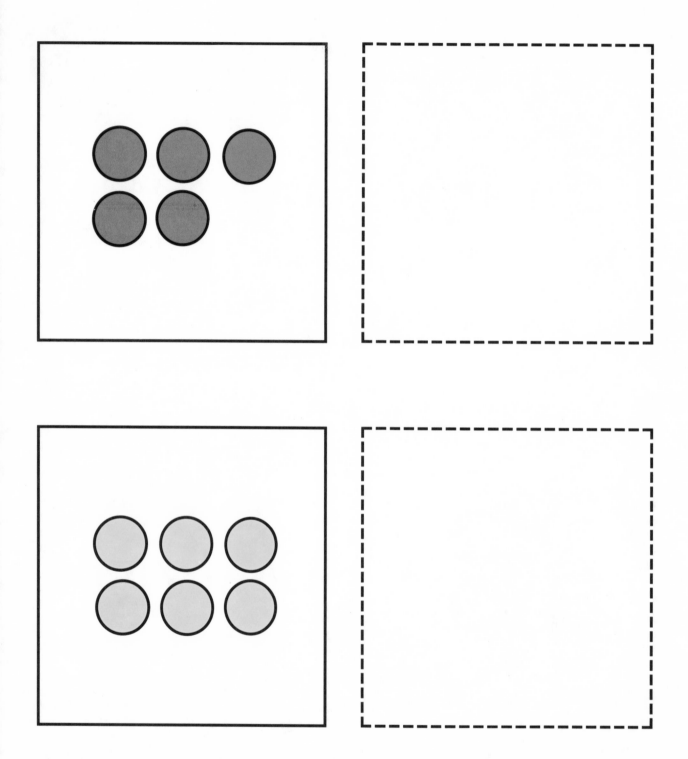

Count the dots in the squares. Can you find the cut-out card with the same number of dots? Place the correct card next to the box.

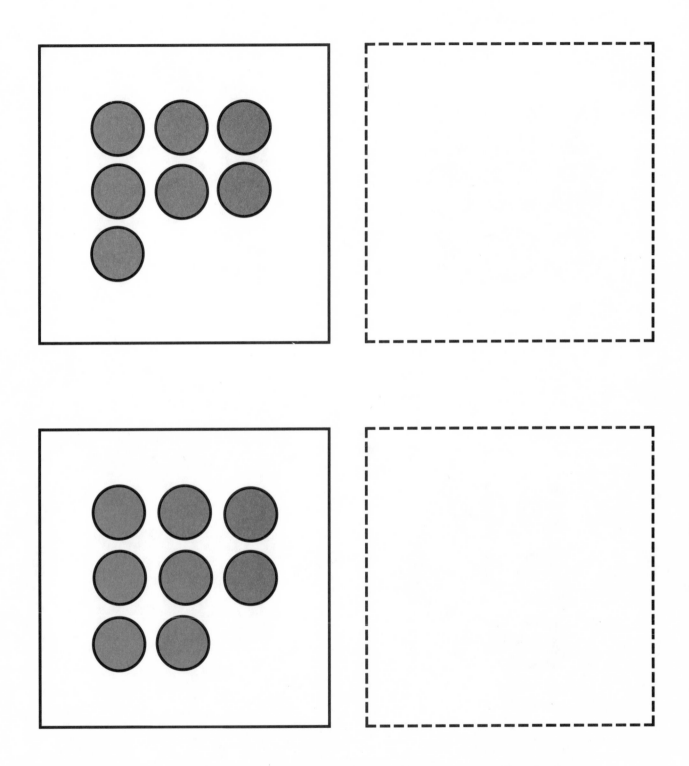

Count the dots in the squares. Can you find the
cut-out card with the same number of dots?
Place the correct card next to the box.

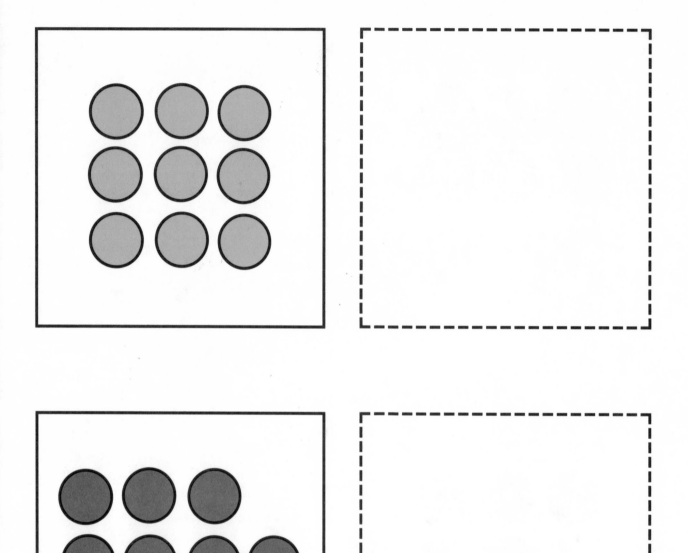

Count the dots in the squares. Can you find the cut-out card with the same number of dots? Place the correct card next to the box.

Connect the Dots

Can you connect the dots in order from 1 to 10 to form a picture?

More Numbers Fun

Here are additional activities you can do with your child to help him or her learn numbers.

• Have your child look for numbers all around you. Point out the numbers on clocks, telephones, street signs, license plates, and price tags.

• Let your child help fold the laundry by matching pairs of socks.

• Make a fruit salad with your child and count all the ingredients as you use them. Use 1 bowl, 2 mixing spoons, 3 raspberries, 4 blueberries, 5 orange slices, 6 apple slices, 7 grapes, 8 banana slices, 9 strawberries, and 10 raisins.

• Let your child put together the three number puzzles using the cut-out cards. Mix up the cards with 1, 2, 3, and 4 in the upper corner and ask your child to put the cards in order to see the picture of the tool belt. Do the same thing with the cards numbered 5, 6, 7, and 8 so your child can see the picture of the tea party scene. The cards numbered 9 and 10 form a school bus.

• Have your child match the numbers on the manipulatives with the numbers on pages 3-12.

• Take nature walks and collect leaves, rocks, acorns, or anything else you like. Help your child count and sort objects into sets. Your collections can be sorted into sets by color, size, shape, and even texture.

Manipulatives

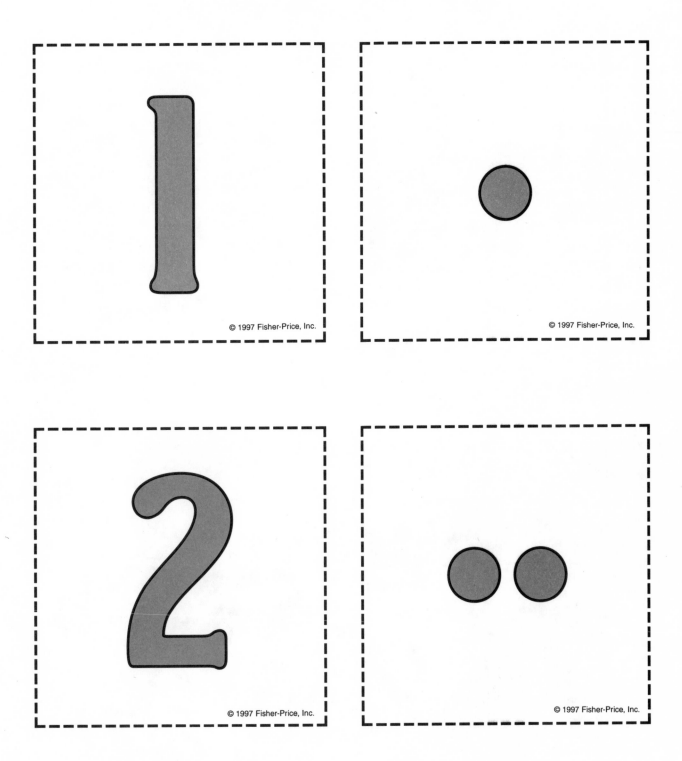

© 1997 Fisher-Price, Inc.

© 1997 Fisher-Price, Inc.

© 1997 Fisher-Price, Inc.

© 1997 Fisher-Price, Inc.

Cut out these cards for your child to use with selected activities.

1.

© 1997 Fisher-Price, Inc.

© 1997 Fisher-Price, Inc.

2.

© 1997 Fisher-Price, Inc.

© 1997 Fisher-Price, Inc.

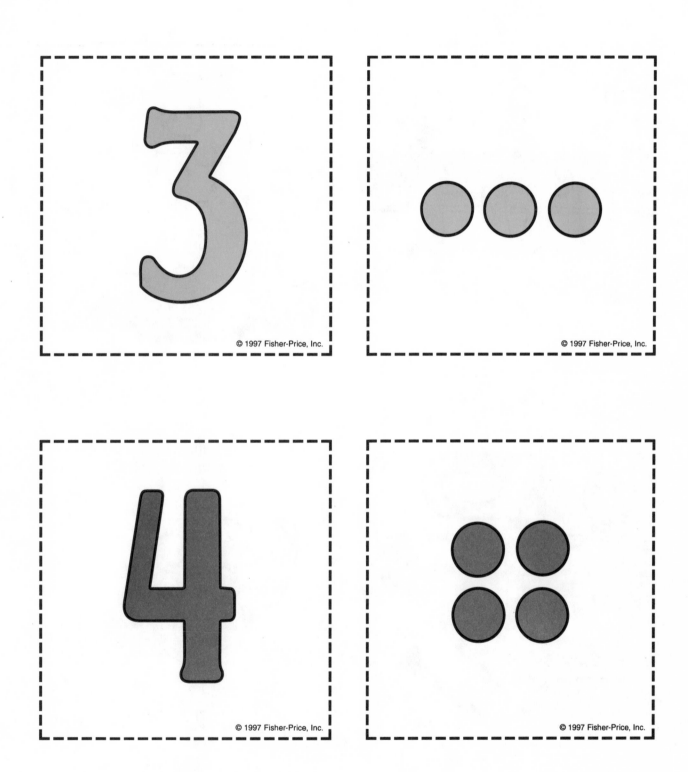

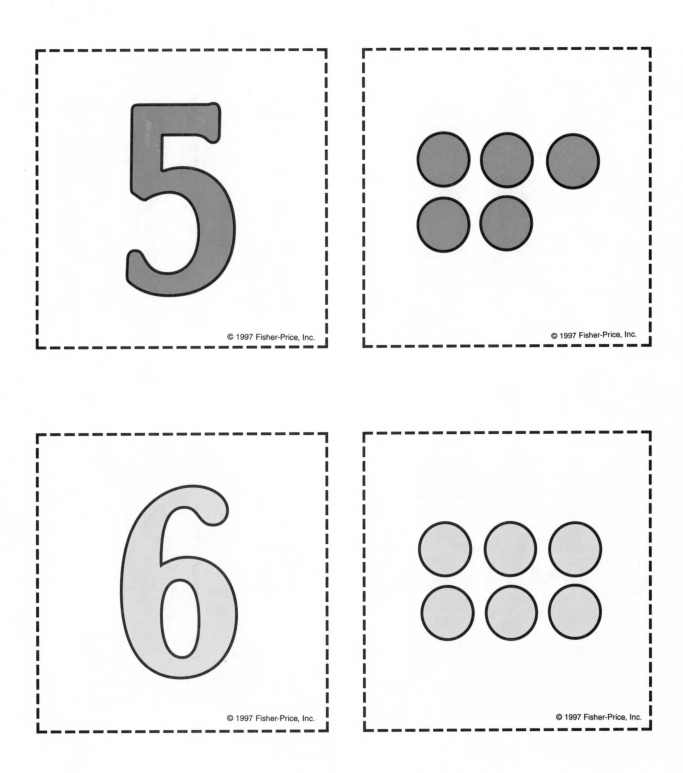

© 1997 Fisher-Price, Inc.

© 1997 Fisher-Price, Inc.

© 1997 Fisher-Price, Inc.

© 1997 Fisher-Price, Inc.

5.

6.

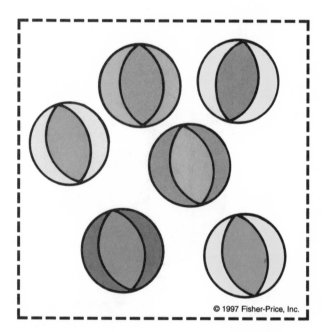

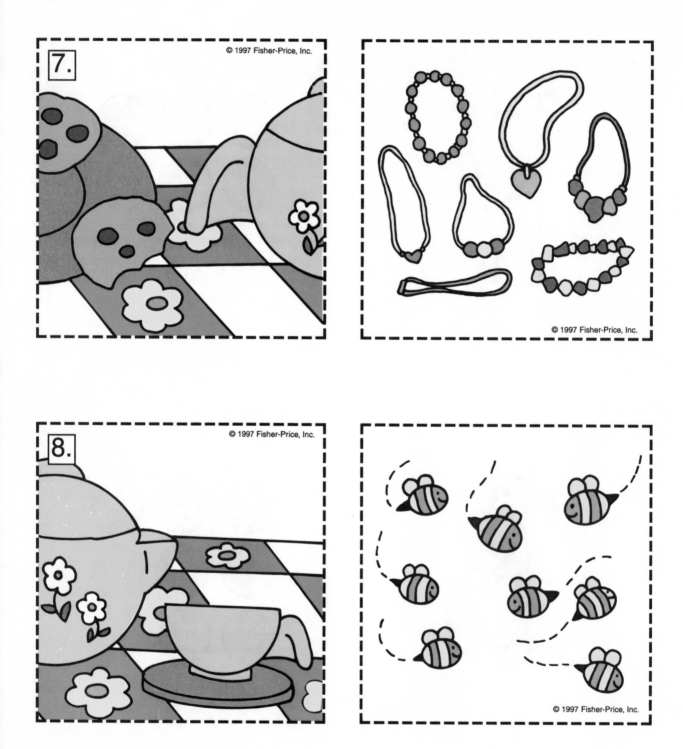

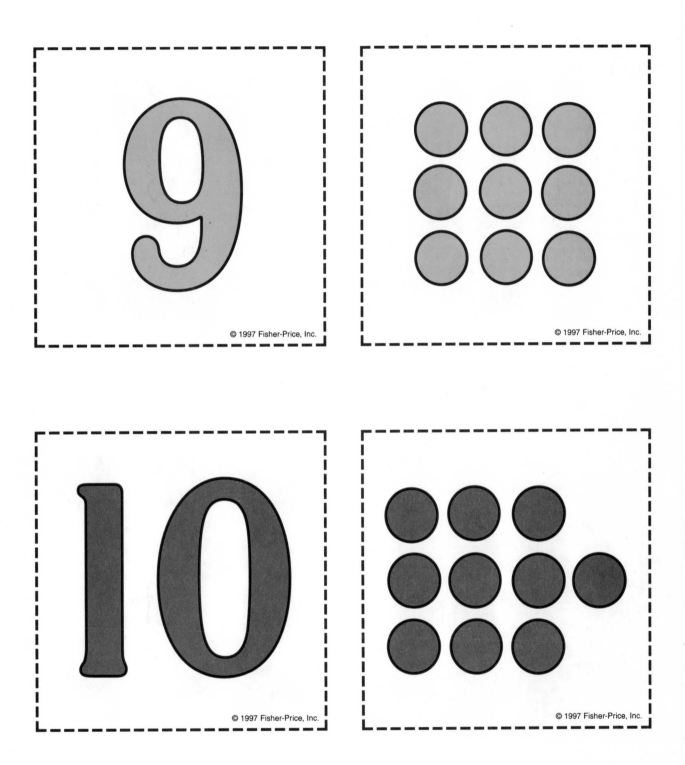